1

The Book of What's in Hell

A New Kingdom Guide to the World of the Dead

Hieroglyphic Text
transcribed, transliterated, and annotated by

Jacob Rabinowitz

Table of Contents

Preliminary Note

It is many years since I composed this book, and originally I did so as much for my own convenience as a reader as with any thought of publishing my work for the benefit of Egyptologists. At present I have no one to turn to to copy-edit the Egyptian, so there are unquestionably errors, despite my best efforts. I mention that so that the student will not *immediately* assume that any oddity in this volume indicates a defect in his knowledge, which must be supplied by ransacking the dictionary. It may, alas, be due to the fallible eye of this editor.

This is the companion volume to the English translation and full commentary, which is also available from Amazon. Therein the choices, arrangement, and early termination are fully explained

Hour One:

Going Below the Horizon

Poem of the First Hour

A2h2a jn h2m n nt2r pn
m-h3t h2tp.f r a2rrt tn.
Wd2-mdw n nn n nt2rw jmyw.s:

"Wn n.j sbaw.t2n,
ss2 n.j arrwt.t2n,
stj n.j, jrj.w n.j ss2m,
h3prw m h2a2w.j!
Wd2.n.j t2n—r-t2n—h4at.j;
jrj.n.j t2n m ba.j,
qma.n.j t2n n ah3w.j.

"Jj.n.j nd2.j-h3r.j jm.j,
snf.j h2a2w.j, a2h2a2.sn.
Jw.j sh2tm.j jryw r.s,
dj.j srq, m sfg-jrw,[1]
Wsjr-H3nty-Jmntyw.

---

1 Taking *Sfg* as "mysterious; abnormal" (*cf.* Sethe on Pyramid Text 655a). The Epithet refers to Ra, not Osiris, and is paralleled a few lines later in the reply of the gods with *s2ta jrw*.

"Wn n.j a2wy.t2n, bntyw!
Sns2 n.j a2rrt.t2n, bntyw!
Nt2rwt.j h3prwt m ba.j, nt2rw:
h3pr.t2n, h3pr.t2n n H3prj-h3nty-Dwat.
A2ha2.t2n n Wr-n-s,
mny.t2n n jdb s2ta,
jrj.t2n n dwatyw r a2rrt.
Jr.t2n, m st.t2n ah2wt n.t2n nt sh3wt.t2n."

Nt2rw a2rrt tn n Ra2, snsj.sn nt2r a2a:

"Wn n.k Jmnt, s2ta jrw,
sns2 n.k wnwy Njwt Wrt,
sh2d2 n.k kkyt,
srq.k h2tmyt
ja2r.k m rn.k n Ra
r bw h4ry Wsjr-H3nty-Jmntyw.

12

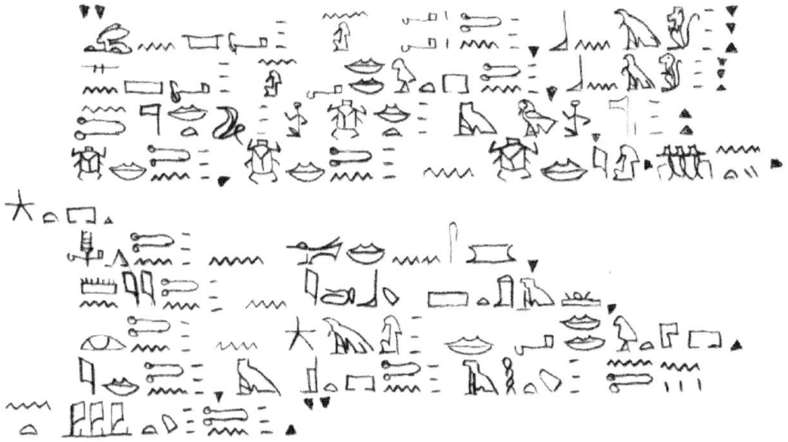

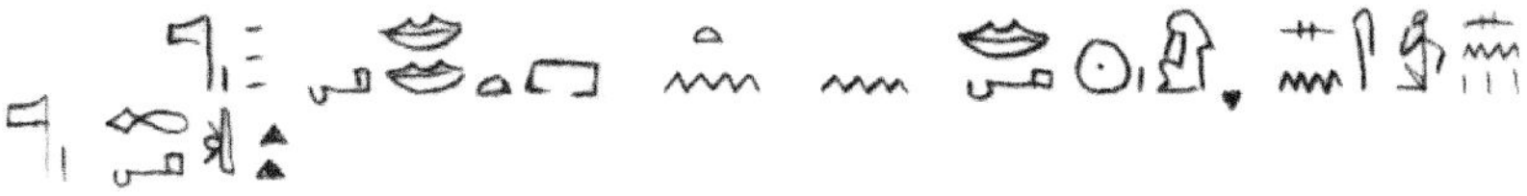

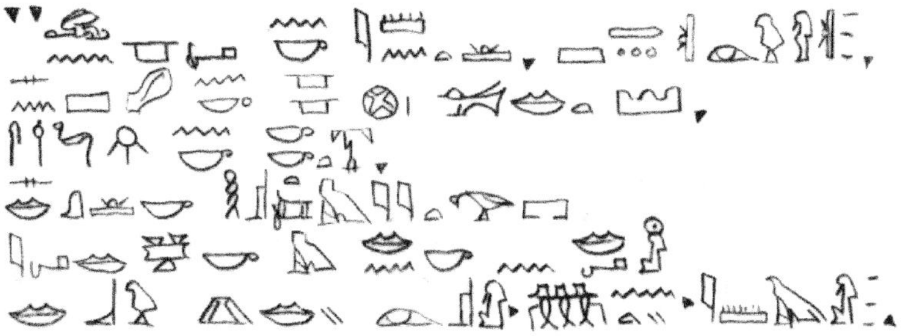

"Jw hy n Ra2 r r wnwy ta,
jaw n.k, srq ah3w,
a2q.k r sba n Wrt,
wn.n n.k wnwy m bntyw,
wn.n n.k m ht2tw,
snsj t2w snsywt.k,
sh2d2 n.k ah3wt.k kkw,
dwa t2w nt2rw.k, Ra2,
ss2m t2w wnwt jmywt.k,
st2a t2w saty.ky m wja.k,
h2tp.k, wd2w tpyw sh3wt ta,
jt2jt.k: grh; jnjt.k: hrw.

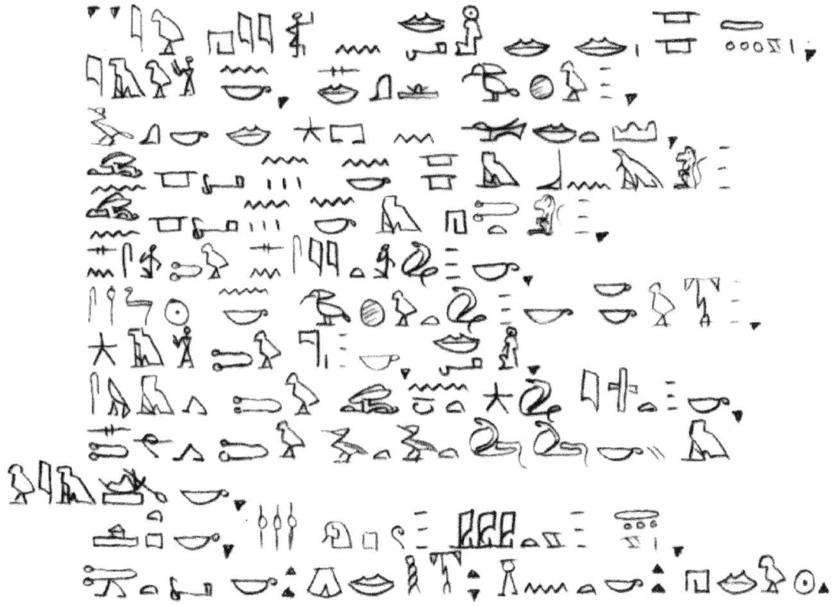

"Twt nt2r pw wd2a wnwt,
htp.k m wja H3prj,
jt2a.n.k tpyw h2bntt {mms2}.
H2tp n.k Njt, wpj.k nt r gs.k;[2]
kfj n.k D2ba2-Ta rmn.f.
Jaj tw nt2rwt Wr-n-s,
jaj n.k h2nwyt,
smaa2-h3rw.k r h3ftyw.k,
dj.k sd2b m njkw."

Wd2-mdw jn h2m n nt2r pn a2a m-h3t spr a2rrt tn:

---

2 Taking the owl as a mistaken reading of *m* for *gs*.

"A2h2a.n a2rrwt.tn,
rwd2.n wnw.t2n,
h3tm.n qarwt.t2n,
jyw h3r.j n a2pw—
h3r.j n s2asw.j:
mn{.n}.t2n m swt.t2n,
a2h2a2w r jdb.t2n."

A2pp nt2r pn h2r.sn, hwt.sn,
m-h3t snn.f sn (n) Wr-n-s.

Introduction to the First Hour:

Ss2 n a2t jmnt; a2h2a2w baw,
nt2rw, s2wt, ah3w; jrw;
h2at: wpt jmntt, sba n ah3t jmntt;
ph2wy: kkw sma(w), sba n ah3t jmntt;
rh3 baw datyw, rh3 jrw,
rh3 sah3.sn n Ra2;
rh3 baw, s2taw!
rh3 jmyt wnwt nt2rw.sn;
rh3 dwj(w).f n.sn, rh2 sbaw wawt
a2ppt nt2r a2a h2r.sn,
rh3 s2mt wnwt nt2r.sn,
rh3 was2yw h2tmyw.

A2q nt2r pn m a2rrt jmntt n ah3t, a2h2a2 Sth3 r jdb;
jtrw s2t-md2wy ph2rt a2rrt tn n sprt wja datyw;
a2pp.f m h3t r Wr-n-s.

Pictures and Commentary

Complete Image of the First Hour

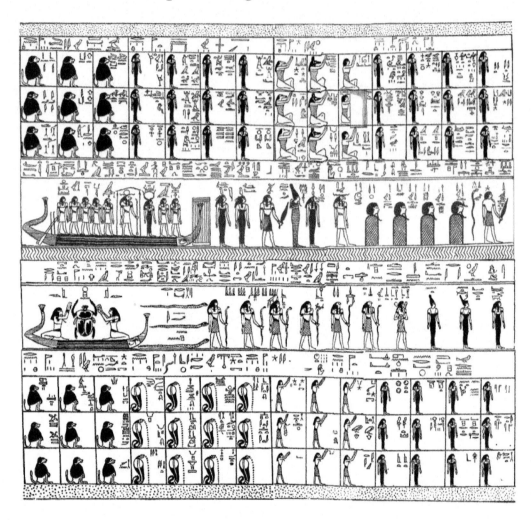

The Boat of the Sun Preceded by Maat

Maa2t-Maa2t, Wpj-Wawt, Sja, Nbt-Wja, Jwf, H2r-H2knw, Ka-Maa2t, Nhs, H2w, H3rp-Wja;

Ra's Guardians

Nknw, H3nty-Jmntt, Sh3mt, Sh2dw Wr;

Four Steles and Traveler

Wd2-Mdw Ra2, Wd2-Mdw Jtm, Wd2-Mdw H3prj, Wd2-Mdw Wsjr; D2aj-Wnwt;

Second Level of the Middle Register

Kepri Boat

Wsjr-H3prj-Wsjr; Sk-R, Sf, Spd;

Harvest Spirits

Sh3ty, Smwy, Bnbnty; H2bnw, Mdwy, D2awty, H2bnty;

Neith and her Entourage

Njt, A2rt, Nbt-H2wt, Wpj-Nt, D2ba-Ta.

Text in the Middle Registers

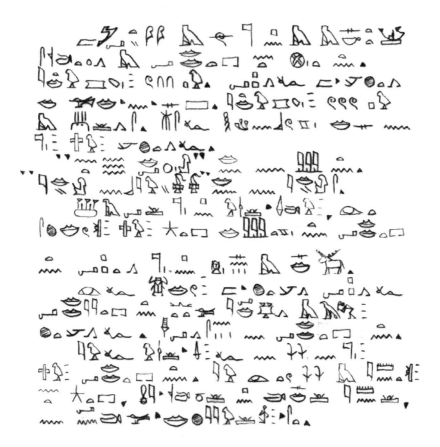

Ma2aty m st2a nt2r pn m Msktt sqdjt m a2rrt nt njwt tn.

Jtrw s2t md2wy pw. App.f m h3t r Wr-n-s. Jtrw h3mt s2t pw m aw.s. Ms
h2nb r.s n nt2rw jmyw h3t.f.

"Nt-Ra" rn n sh3t tn. "Jrj Nbjwy" rn n jry.s.

S2aa2 nt2r pn wd2-mdw, jrjt sh3rw jmyw Dat r sh3t tn a2rrt tn a2ppt nt2r
pn h2r.sn m sr.

Jrj(r).f h3prw m-h3t a2pp.f a2rrt tn jwtt ja2r mtyw h3t.f. A2ha2.sn n a2rrt
tn. Jw.f wd2-mdw.f n nn n nt2rw jmyw a2rrt tn. Jw jrj.tw nn m jmnt nt dwat,
mj-qd
pn dsr jmn, n a2nd-rh3yw-st.

Upper and Lower Registers

Upper Register

Earth Openers

Rnw nw nt2rw wnyw n ba a2a:
Bntj, Jwf, {Dh2dh2},
Jb-Ta, Jbjb-Ta, H2knw,
Wn-Ta, Wba-ta, Ma-n-Ra2.

Praising Goddesses

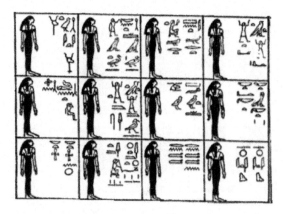

Rnw nw nt2rwt snsywt Jmy Ta:
H2tyt, H2wnt, Nbt A2nh3,
H2knt-m-Ba.s, Qajt-m-Ah3.s, Sh3mt-m-H3ftyw.s
Jmnt Wrt, S2fyt, {R Nt2t2}
Qajt-a2, Nbt Mkt, {Sh4jt}.

Adoring Gods

Rnw nw nt2rw dwayw Ra2:

D2aj Dwat, Ngy, Sh3m H2r,
Nb Ta D2sr, {Wpj Tawy, Wpj Sh3mty,}
{H2d2 A2, Maa A2}, H2sj A2.

Goddesses Who Lead Ra

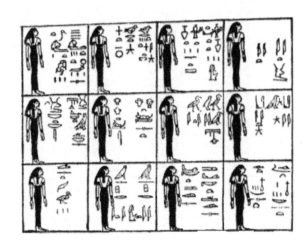

Rnw nw nt2rwt ss2mywt nt2r a2a:
Ws2mt-h2awt-h3ftyw.s, Ss2at-mkjt-nb.s, Dnt-baw,
Wrt-jmyt-Dat, H2ryt-Jb-Wja.s, Mspryt,
H3sft-Smayt-Sth4, Ws2awt, Mkjt Nb.s,
Dndyt, Sbayt, Maat-Nfrw-Nb.s

Lower Register

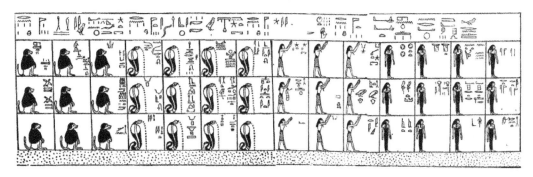

Praising Baboons

Rnw nw nt2rw h2syw n Ra2 a2q.f m Dwat:
Ht2t, Pat2t2, Bsj,
H2kn-m-Bsy.f, Jba, (anon.)
Jmy-Kar, H3nty-Ta, {H2nn}.

Cobra Goddesses

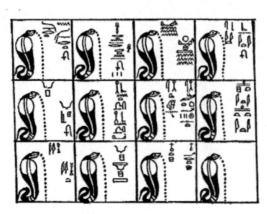

Rnw nw nt2rwt sh2d2ywt kkw m Dwat:
Nsrt, Wpst, Wad2t,
Mrt-Nsrt, Bh2nt, Wps2t,
H3wjt-Taw, H2sqt-H3ftyw, Nfrt-H3aw,
Bsjt, H2tpyt, (anon.)

Praising Gods

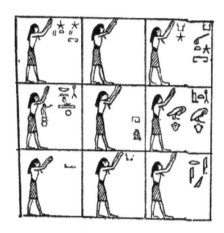

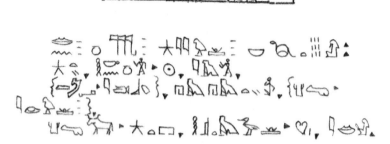

Rnw nw nt2rw dwayw nb psd2t:
Dwaty, H2knw-Ra2, Jaj,
{Maa2-Jdb}, Hmhmty, {Ka-Jrw},
Ka-Dwat, H2tmw-Jb, Jry.

Praising Goddesses

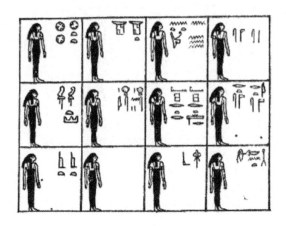

Rnw nw Nt2rwt ddwt hnw n Ra2 m a2pjw Wr-n-s:
Njwtyt, Jmntyt, Ast,
Nbt-H2wt, {H2r.sy}, (anon.)
Ntyt, A2prt-R, Jabyt,
Maat-Nt2r.s, Jryt-Nt2r.s, H2knt.

Postscript

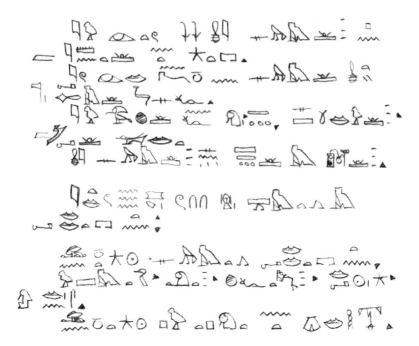

Jw jrj.tw nn mj ss2m pn m jmnt nt Dwat.
Jw jrj nw n ss2m mjty nt2r a2a d2s.f.
Jw a2h3 n.f tp-ta, ss2rw maa2 wrt
mj ss2m.sn s2ta m ss2.

Jtwr s2t mdwy h2r s2mt m a2rrt tn;
wnwt ss2mt a2rrt tn,
Ws2m-H2awt-H3ftyw-Ra2 rn.s.
Wnwt pw tpt nt grh2.

Hour Two:

Realm of the Buried Seeds

Poem of the Second Hour

D2d-mdw jn nt2rw dwatyw h3ft nt2r pn a2a
a2q.f m "A2m-r-Dr," h4nj.f "Nt-Ra" r "Wr n.s:"

"J h3aj, ba a2a, ss2p(w).n n.s dwat, jwf jry pt,
r a2nh3.k, Jwf, m ta d2sr n.k.

"Mj jr.k Ra2{.k}, m rn.k m "Anh3w, H3prj H3nty Dwat,"
h3ns.k sh3wt, h3wjw, jnt2.k hjw, hwj.k "Nh2a-H2r!"

"Jw hy m pt hnw m ta n wba h4at.f.
Hd2, sh2d2 wrw h2ay jmy tp Ra2,
dr kkw m a2t jmnt m rn.k n "H3sr S2tw-A2!"³
Hd2 kkw smaw anh3 jwf mawj.f h3r.f

———————————
3 Lit. "mysterious of limb."

"H2tp wy Ra2 m Jmntt, wja.k n.k;
ma2a wy ss2m tw, h4nww.k jmyw ta;
a2.sn s2ta n h2tm.sn n.k A2pp r wnt "Mkt Nb.s."

"Jaw sp-sn, sbj(w) n ba.f, s2as(w) apr(w), jj n h4t.f.
Wpj, {akwt}, wn a2awy ta. S2taw, s2mt.k m Wsjr!
Nd2.tw.k, nd2.tw Wsjr, ma2a-h3rw.k r h3ftyw.k.
M-h2tp sp-sn n Jmnt m H3prj, m H3prj n{n} Jabtt."

Wd2-mdw jn h2m n nt2r pn a2a
n nt2rw dwatyw h3ntyw "Wr n.s:"

"Wn sbaw.t2n s2taw, maa jwf.j, kfj kkw.t2n!
mw n.t2n n "Wr n.s," rwj.tw t n.t2n n rdt jm,

t2aw n.t2n, n h2tm.t2n, ss2rt n snt2w.t2n, n d2w stj h2waat.t2n,
ss2.n wtaw.t2n, dwn.n rdwy.t2n, s2m.t2n h2r.sn, pd2 nmtt.t2n;
{t2n} n.t2n baw.t2n, n h2r.sn r.t2n,
a2nh3 jrw.t2n mdw.sn ah3w.t2n.

"Spd.n sftw.t2n qnj.t2n h3ftyw Wsjr:
mn trw.t2n, d2dt n rnpwt.t2n,
h3pr h3prw n wnwt.t2n,
hms.t2n {jkawt.t2n,} bdt n.t2n m t, kamwt n.t2n m ma2a-h3rw.

"Naj.t2n n wja.j, h2ms.t2n r ss2m{w} sa2nh3 maw sh3wt!
Ntt2n sh3tyw "Wr n.s," a2nh3w, ba(w), jmyw.j.

Ntt2n a2h2a(w) h2r h2a2w.j, mkjw wj r A2pp;
a2nh3.t2n n ba.j, srq.t2n n h4at.j,
mn.t2n n st.t2n dsrt wd2t n.t2n wnn.t2n jm.s.

"Jw.j a2n hrw, h3tw.j m dwat, sbj.j grh2 h3sr.j kkw
{jmj.t2n wj} s2m.j m-h3t ah3t.j, sbj.j h2r h3tw jabt.j.
Jhy, dwatyw, nd2.j t2n! Jhy, jrj.j sh3rw.t2n!

D2wj.n.sn (n) nt2r pn m h2pt wja.f jmy ta;
hwt.sn, sbj.n.f sn r h2tp m sh3t Nprtyw jmyw m-h3t Wsjr

Prose Introduction to the Second Hour

H2pt m "Wr n.s" jn nt2r pn, jrjt-h2pwt[4] Jarw m "Nt-Ra2:" jtrw h3mt-s2t psd2 m aw n sh3t tn, s2t md2wy m wsh3.s: jr(r) nt2r pn a2a h2nbwt n nt2rw r njwt tn. Rn n wnt nt grh2 s2mst nt2r pn a2a:
"S2sat Mkjt Nb.s." Rn n sba n njwt tn: "A2m r D2r."

H2nb nt2r pn a2a ah2wt n nt2rw dwatyw, jrr.f sh3rw.sn r sh3t tn.

Rh3 dwatyw! Jr rh3 rnw.sn, wn.f h3r.sn,
h2nb n.f nt2r pn aa2 ah2wt r bw.sn n sh3t Wr-n-s, a2h2a2.f h3r a2h2a2w Ba,
app.f m-h3t nt2r pn a2a, a2q.f ta, wba.f Dwat, wpj.f sbt m h2kntyw,[5]
a2pp.f h2r A2mw-A2a m-h3t Maa2t H2nbyw.

1)

2)

---

4   We would expect the plural rather in the idiom *d2sr h2pwt* (handle the rudder), but it is quite acceptable as a variation on *jrj h2pt*.

5   Literally: "He will shave the hair from the shaggy ones, it is following Truth-of the-Field-Measure that he passes by the donkey eater." The overall sense of these obscure characters seems by context clear. The shaggy ones are demons who attack the guilty, and the equation of hair with power is evident from the long beard which is a royal emblem of power (*cf.* the hair of Samson.) The donkey is an animal closely associated with Seth, and so comes to be used as a synonym for sinner (*cf.* the parallel Christian metaphor of the goat.)

Jw.f wnm.f t r Wja-Ta, dj.tw n.f h2att Ta-Tbj Wja.[6]

Jw jrj.tw nn ss2mw n(w) baw Dwat m ss2,
mj qd pn, m jmnt nt Dwat — h2at-jmnt.
Jw ph4r.n.tw(.sn) n.sn tp ta m rnw.sn.
Jw ah3 n s tp-ta — maa2 h2h2 n sp.

---

6 *Ta-Tbj* (spelled here *Ta-Twb*): an earth god mentioned in P.T. 560. *Tbj* itself remains obscure. Probably little more is in play here than an archaic-poetic term for earth.

Complete Image of the Hour

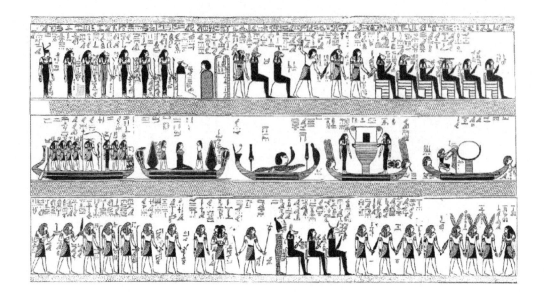

Boat of Ra

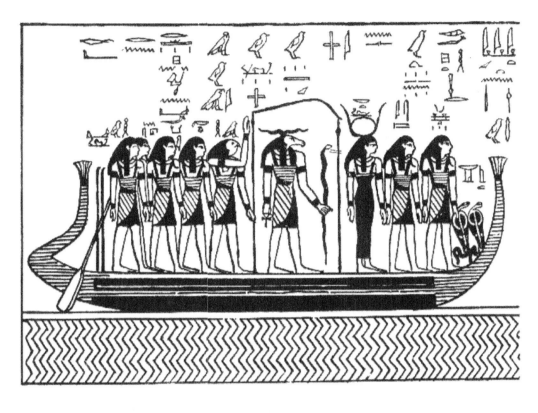

Wja-n-Ra2: Ast, Nbt-H2wt, Wpj-Wawt, Sja, Nbt-Wja, Jwf, H2r-H2knw, Ka-Maa2t, Nhs, H2w, H3rp-Wja.

Boat of Grain

Wja-H4nj-Nt, Npr, Npr, Jat Kamwtt.

Crocodile Boat

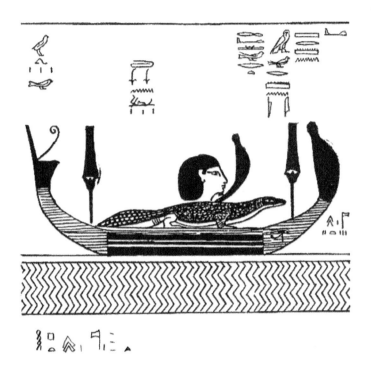

H2pt Nt2rw.

Hathor Boat

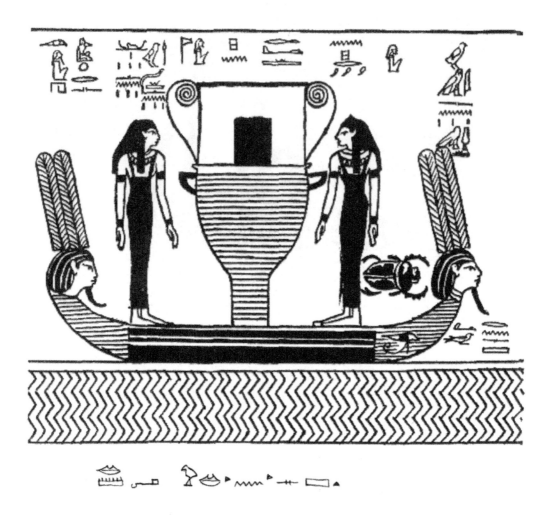

Rmnjw Wr-n-s.

Thoth Boat

Dpw Dwatyw, Rmnj Maa2t.

Text in the Middle Register

The text is lost.

Upper Register

Upper Register

The Nine Goddesses of the Hour

*Maa2t Tpyt Jnt, H2d2t Tpyt Jnt, Nt Tpyt Jnt,
Jmnt Nfrt, A2mt D2rw, Sh3mt Wasyt,
H2ryt Tpyt Dwatyw, A2mt Mtw, Msjt-Sy-D2s.s.*

Psyche of Ra

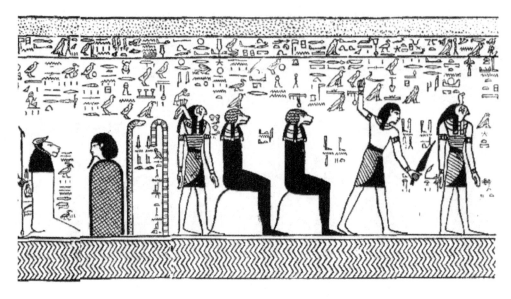

Ssnd2t Ah3w, Wd2-Mdw n Wsjr, Mdw n Wsjr, Mst n Wsjr, Hrwy.fy, Ja2n, Bntj, Sbn-H2sq-S2wt, H2r Dwaty, Sh3m-A2-Hwj-H3ftyw.f.

College of Judges

Ktjwtyt-Dnt-Baw, Jwf-h2ry-H3ndw.f, D2h2wty-h2ry-H3ndw.f, H4nmw Qnbty, Gb Qnbty, Ast Nd2t.

Text in the Upper Register

Wnn.sn m sh3r pn: jw.sn dwa.sn n nt2r pn a2a m-h3t spr.f r.sn.
Jn h3rw.sn ss2m sw r.sn. Jn hwt.sn sbb sw m-h3t wd2.f n.sn mdw.
Jn nn n nt2rw sa2r mdw tpyw-ta. Ntsn sa2r baw r qdd.sn.
Jrjt.sn pw sh3pr jnw ws2aw, jrj.t(w) h3rywt r wnwt.sn.
Ntsn saw hrw, jnn grh2 r prjt nt2r pn a2a
m kkw smaw r h2tp m a2rrt nt ah3t jabtt nt pt.
Jw.sn hwt.sn n nt2r pn a2a, jakb.sn n.f m-h3t a2pp.f h2r.sn.
Jw rh3 sn, m prj-m-hrw, jt2j.tw.f m grh2 r jmaw njwt wrt.

Lower Register

Spirits of Harvest-Time

Wpj Trw, Jry Trw, Fajw, A2 Fajw.

Spirits of the Harvest

Rnpty, Mah3y, Nh2rw.

Aspects of Sirius

Hd2d2wty, H2wn Wr, H2d Wr.

Psyche of Osiris

H2rwy.fy-A2wy.fy-m-H2nw.f, Ah3y, Wsjr-Wnn-Nfr.

Judges of the Dead

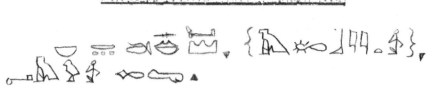

Nb Ta D2sr, {Ah4byt}, A2mw A2a.

Reapers and Guardian

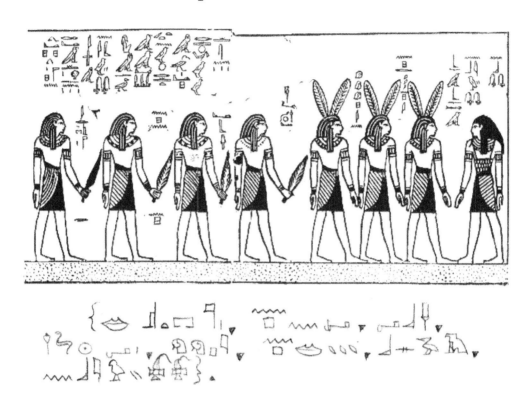

{Jrj St Nt2r, Npn(t), A2ba, H2d2-A2, Tp Tpy, Npr, Bsa, Nbjwy}.

Text in the Lower Register

Wnn.sn m sh3r pn
h2nk.sn n nt2r pn a2a m trw,
h2nk.sn n.f rnpwt jmy(w)t a2wy.sn.

Jw nt2r pn a2a,
wd2.f n.sn mdw d2wj.sn n.f:
a2nh3.sn m h3rw nt2r pn a2a,

srq h2tywt.sn d2wj.f sn, wd2.f sn jryw.sn,
maa2.f n.sn smw jmyw sh2wt.sn.

Ntsn snm wad2d2t jmyt Wr-n.s n nt2rw jmyw h3t Ra2, ntsn
ja2b mw n ah3w, wd2(w) nt2r pn a2a, ntsn rkh2 wawat r
samt h3ftyw nw Ra2,
ntsn wdd h2atyw h2r sd2ty,
hwt.h3r.sn, jaqb.sn m-h3t a2pp nt2r pn a2a h2r.sn.

"Jmy Nbjwy" m sawty sh3t tn.
Jw rh3 st m ah3 a2pr(w) h3wjw.sn.

Post-Script

Jw jrj.tw nn my ss2m pn m jmnt nt a2t.
Jw rh3 mdw pn m a2r h3r dwatyw.
Jw ah3 n s tp-ta: ma2a s(t).

Wnt tn: "S2sat-Mkjt-Nb.s."

Hour Three:

Ghost World

Poem of the Third Hour

D2d-mdw n nt2rw s2taw

h3ft nt2r pn a2a a2q.f m "Jt2jw,"
h4nj.f nt "Nb Wa2 Dj H3pr{t} Awt":

"Mj r.k n.n, h4nnw jwf.f, ss2mw n h2a2w.f d2s.f, aa2a2jw Dwat, nb srq mdw, jrj a2nh3.f.

"H3a2j ba.k, was2 sh3m.k, ss2m t2w Ma2aty.ky m wat kkw, pt n ba.k, ta n h4at.k,

a2h2a2 n.k Wa2t wa2tyt n nfrt mnjt sabw,[7] s2sp t2w a2wy jmntyw m jrw.k d2sr n "Nh3h3."

---

7   Lit.: "at the ship's bow-rope which (relative verb) jackals pull along."

"Nfr wy m maa jmntyw, h2tp wy m sd2m jmntyw Ra2 m h2pt.f m jmntt, h2d2wt.f m kkw ss2mw.[8]

Mj r.k n.n, Ra2 ah3ty, H3prj nbw, {mw nt2r}.

H4nj.k jdbw dwat, h3ns.k sh3wt.k jmnt: h3pr.k hprwt m ta.k pw.

Rnn n.k njwt wrt, h2tp n.k h2r.s {m-a2 h2kn jr.k n} Wsjr h2kn.f n.k m d2t.f jmyt dwat:

Ha Ra2 ma2a-h3rw! Ha Ra2 h2wj h3ftyw.f! Maa2-h3rw.k Ra2 r h3ftyw.k nb(w), jtn h2d2, ba sh2d2 ta."

D2d-mdw jn h2m (n) nt2r pn a2a n baw s2taw jmyw h3t Wsjr:

(five lines corrupt)

---

8   Lit.: "in the darkness of forms."

{five lines obsc.}

"J ah3w Wsjr, jmyw h3t h3nty jmntyw,
mn n jrw.t2n, ah3 n h3prw.t2n, ssnt-t2aw n fndw.t2n, maa n h2rw.t2n, sd2m n
sd2mw.t2n, kfjt n a2fnwt.t2n, wh2a2 n wtw.t2n,
h2tpw n.t2n tpy-ta, mw n.t2n n nprwt nt2r, ah2wt n.t2n n sh3wt.t2n.
Nn h3r baw.t2n, nn sh3d h4awt.t2n.
Wn n sbaw.t2n, ss2p n qrrwt.t2n, a2h2a2 n.t2n h2r swt.t2n!

"Jj.n.j a2a r maa h4at.j, sjp.j ss2m.j jmy dwat, h4nnw Ta-Tnn h4nnw.j, aw-a2w
jrj.sn h2pt.j; ba.k n pt, Wsjr; h4at.k n ta, h3nty Jgrt;
nt2rw.k m-h3t.k, ah3w.k tp a2wy.k, h3pr.n twtw.k jmyw.k. Jst2 ah3 n ah3.k,
Wsjr; ah3 n ah3w.t2n jmyw h3t Wsjr . . ."
(three lines corrupt).

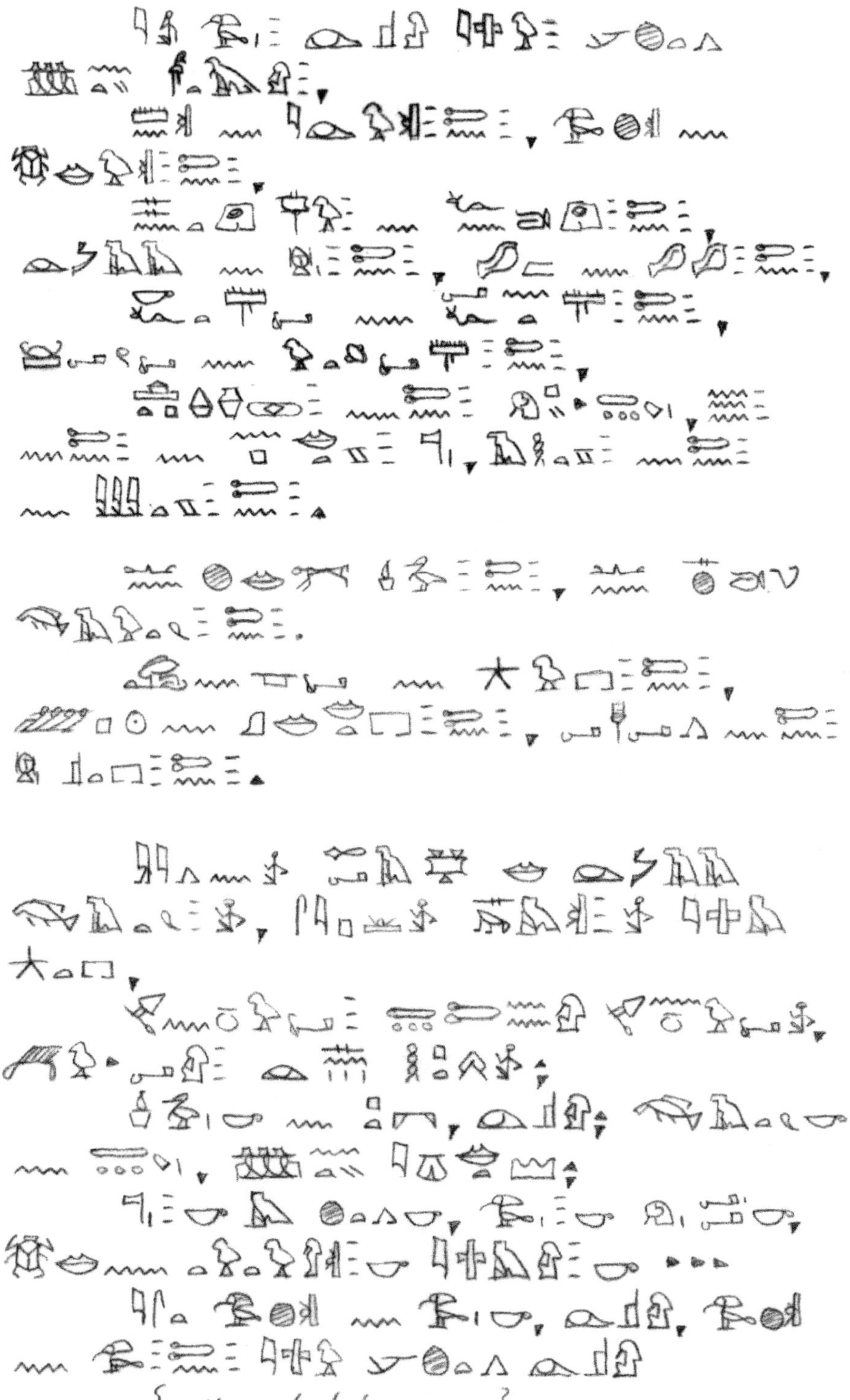

{ three last lines obsc. }

Introduction

H2pt m sh3t nprtyw jn h2m n nt2r pn a2a, jrjt h2pwt m nt Wsjr, (jtrw h3mt s2t psd2 m aw n sht tn,)
wd2.h3r nt2r pn a2a mdw n ah3w jmyw-h3t Wsjr r njwt tn.
Rn n wnwt nt grh2 ss2mt nt2r pn a2a: "Dnt Baw," rn n sba n njwt tn "Jt2j."

Jrj nt2r pn a2a sh3rw nt2rw jmyw h3t Wsjr, wd2.f n.sn h2nb r sh3t tn. Rh3 baw s2taw! Jr rh3 rnw.sn tp-ta,
jw.f a2r.f r bw h4r Wsjr jm, dj.tw n.f mw r sh3t.f tn {tw}.
"Nt Nb Wa2 Dj H3pr Awt" rn n sh3t tn.

Jw jrj.tw nn ss2mw n(w) baw s2taw my qd pn nty m ss2 m jmnt n(t) dwat, h2at {ss2} r jmnt{tyw}. Jw ah3 n s tp-ta, m h4rt-ntr — ss2rw ma2a.

Complete Image of the Hour

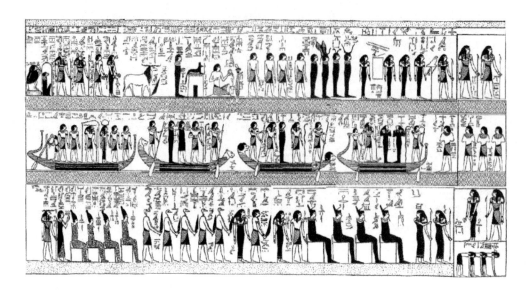

Middle Register

Sun Boat

Wpj Wawt, Sja, Nbt Wja, Jwf, H2r H2knw, Ka Maa2t, Nhs, H3rp Wja.

Floating Bier

Pa H3t: anon.,[9] Stj m Jrt.f, Nb Was, Sfj, Jmy Ta, H4njw.

---

9   We can assume that this rower bears the same unambitious title as his fellow in the
    stern.

84

Dawn Boat

Wja Ht2t: H4nj n.Wrd.f, Stj m H2r.f, anon., anon., Mawt,[10] *Ds m H2r.f.*

---

10 The word means both "newness" and "brightness."

Midnight Boat

Wja A2pr(w): anon., Tka(w) H2r, Bjk{t}, Bjk{t}, A2h2a2w Ss2mw H2r.[11]

---

11   Best reading of a wildly variant text.

Dock Crew

Nb Nt, Mny (r) Ta, Jrj D2rw, Maa D2rw.

Text in the Middle Register

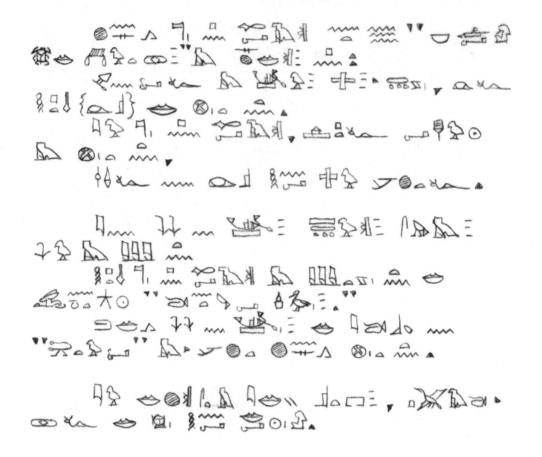

H3ns nt2r pn a2a nt "Nb Wa2 H3pr Awt" (m) sh3r pn:
h4nj.f m wjaw jmyw-ta, jrj.f-h2pt {Wsjr} r njwt tn.
Jw nt2r pn a2a, h2pt.f a2h2a2w m njwt tn, wd2-mdw.f n Wsjr h2na2 jmyw h3t.f.

Jn nn n wjaw s2taw ss2mw sw m sh3t tn
h2pt nt2r pn a2a m sh3t tn r wnwt "Dnt Baw." Ph4r nn n wjaw r jdb n "Jtjw"
m-h3t h3ns njwt tn.

Jw rh3 st m jry swt, pad.f r h2r h2na2 Ra2.

Upper Register

The Journey So Far

Sma H3ftyw, Jnjtt Jnjty, Nhm-H3rw, Jnpw, {Dby,} H2r S2a2j.

Waking the Dead

Wr H2kaw, Jnj D2fd2 Sh2tp Nt2rw, Jnpw n Was, Pd2 A2h2a2.

Canopic Figures

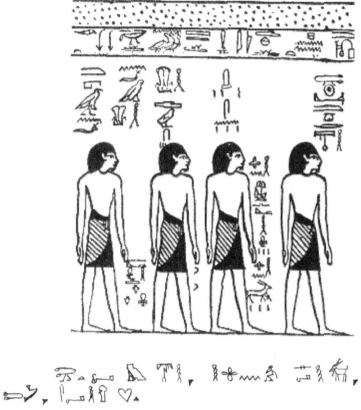

Jt2j m Grh2, H2wn Sa2h2, T2ma, Sa2h2 Jb.

The Mummy

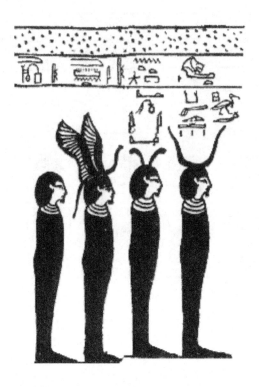

Ba Pf, Ka Jrw, A2way, D2baw.

Mourners

H2ajt, Jakbjt, Mat2ryt, Rmjt.

Horus

Rn.f D2sr{t} m Jmnt, Mh2 Maa2t, Nfrw Nt2rw, {H2r H3tyw}.

Text in Upper Register

Wnn.sn m sh3r pn m dwat, m jwf.sn d2s.sn,

mdwj baw.sn h2r.sn, h2tp s2wwt.sn h2r.sn m-h3t d2wy sn nt2r pn a2a.

Jw.sn mdwj.sn n.f, dwa.sn sw, jakb.sn n.f m-h3t a2pp.f h2r.sn.

Jrjt.sn pw m jmnt: nd2 sbj, sh3pr Nnw, jrjt nmtt H2a2pj.

Prr d2a2 m ta h4r.sn dj.sn h3rw, nd2.sn sbj.

Jw rh3 sn m a2pp h2r.sn, n sbj.n.f n hmhmt.sn, n haj.n.f m h2adw.sn.

Lower Register:

Knum

Nr Ta, H4nmw.

Judges

Wsjr Jt2j H2h2w, Wsjr Sty, Wsjr H3nty Jmntt, Wsjr Nb Jmnt.

Executioners

Dnjwt, Jtmty, anon., Agb(gb).sn, {Nha H2r}.

Damnation

Jmnty, Tpyt Bsw.s, Saa S2a2t, Msh3nt.

Wsjr Sh3m Nt2rw, Wsjr Bjty, Wsjr h2ry H3nw, Wsjr Ka Jmntt.

A2h2aw, Sah2.

New Year

{H3trj}, Bah4yt.

Farewell

S2ta S2m, H2faw, Jakw.[12]

---

12 From the word for "old," *jak* , which has the root-meaning of "bent over, bowed."

Text in the Lower Register

Wnn.sn m sh3r pn dwa.sn nt2r pn a2a. Jw nt2r pn a2a wd2.f n.sn mdw.

A2nh3.sn d2wj.f n sn, wd2.f n.sn mw; s2sp.sn tpw.sn m wd2 tp-r.f.

*Jrjt.sn pw m jmnt: jrjt ma2q s2a2 baw, h3nr swt, rdjt tmw, jwtyw wnn, r st.sn
nt h2tmyt.*

Stt.sn sd2t, sh3pr.sn amwt h3ftyw m jmyt tpw sfw.sn.

Hwt.sn, jakb.sn m-h3t a2pp nt2r pn a2a h2r sn.

{H3trj} rn saa sh3t tn. Jw rh3 st m ba sh3m m rdwy.fy.

Post Script

Jw nt2r pn a2a mnj.f r.sn, {dwj.h3r.f n a2wy wja.f m-h3t wd2.f n.sn mdw.}
Jw jrj.tw mjtt m jmnt nt dwat.
Jw rh2 nn m ah3 sh3m m rdwy.f(y) jwty a2q.f m h2tmyw.
Jw.f prj.f m jrw m hrw, tpj.f t2aw r wnwt.f.
Wnwt ss2mt r sh3t tn "Dnt Baw."

106

Hour Four:

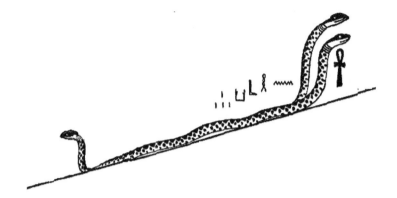

Realm of the Ka

Introduction

H2tp m st2aw jn h2m n nt2r pn a2a m qrrt s2tat nt jmnt "D2srt Jrw."
Jrjt sh3rw ntyw jm.s m h3rw.f jwty maa.f sn.[13]
"Anh3t H3prw" rn n qrrt tn, rn n sba n qrrt tn "Jmn St2aw." Rn n wnwt nt
grh2 ss2mt nt2r pn a2a "Wrt m Sh3m.s."
Jw rh3 ss2m pn m wnm t r r anh3w[14] *m h2wt Jtm.*[15]

---

13 Lit. "by means of his voice, (the voice of him) who does not see them." A bit
    awkward, but quite intelligible. We shall have to make allowances for the enigmatic
    style.

14 Euphemism.

15 The following lines, and many other places in this section, are given in enigmatic
    writing. I have normalized this where the reading is very difficult.

S2taw nw R-St2aw,[16] mt2nw dsrw n Jmh2t, [17]
sbaw jmnw.sn, ta Skr h2ry sa2j.f.
Jrj.tw ss2m pn nty m ss2 m jmn(t) nt dwat h2r jmnt a2t jmnt.
Jw rh3 st, maa2-h3rw, s2m mt2nw R-St2aw, maa ss2m Jmh2t.

---

16   *R-St2aw*, or *Rosetau* as it is usually written out, means literally "the entrance of dragging,"*i.e.*, the mouth of the tomb.

The wheel never really "caught on" in Egypt. Though the Hyksos introduced the chariot in the 17th century BC, its use was confined to the aristocracy, who could afford such sporty and expensive vehicles. The sledge remained the hauler of choice, because of the basic conservatism of the Egyptians, the dominance of Nile boating for all carrying, and because such axeled vehicles as the ancient world could build were not adequate for the heavy stone hauling the Egyptians engaged in.

Thus, in the unwheeled world of Egypt, coffins were always dragged on sledges to the grave, giving us the euphemism "entrance of dragging," — the entrance of the grave to which the coffin is dragged.

17   My translation of *Jmh2t* requires some explanation. The root of the word, *jmh2,*means "to breastfeed," and the term was originally used for an underground source of the Nile. It became a popular name for cemeteries, and in this context one might translate it "Spring of Renewal." Eventually it was used as a general term for the underworld.

In the present book the spelling has been significantly changed. Ordinarily the word has an extra "m," clearly added for sense rather than sound. This second "m" is the flat, abstracted image of the primaeval mound, which reinforces the idea of renewal and rebirth. But in our text both "m"s have been replaced by the arm which is an abbreviated writing of *mj*, the imperative of "to give. There is however no sense of giving. The *h2* remains a braided lamp-wick, and the final *t* is represented by a rope hobble. The image created by the arm and the two cords before is one of restraint and constriction. Thus my rendering of the term as "Deadlock." I have however given it in the non-enigmatic spelling for ease of reading.

Complete Image of the Hour

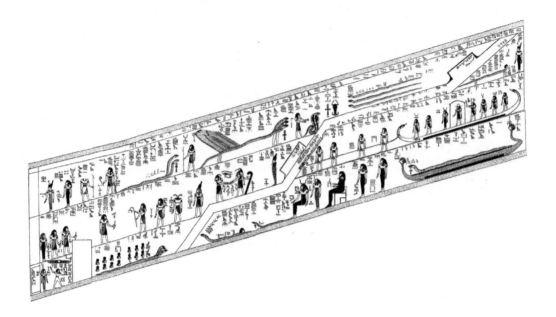

Complete Image: Left

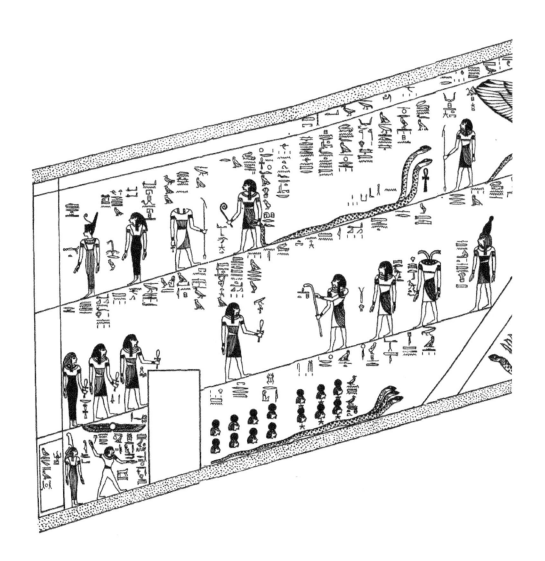

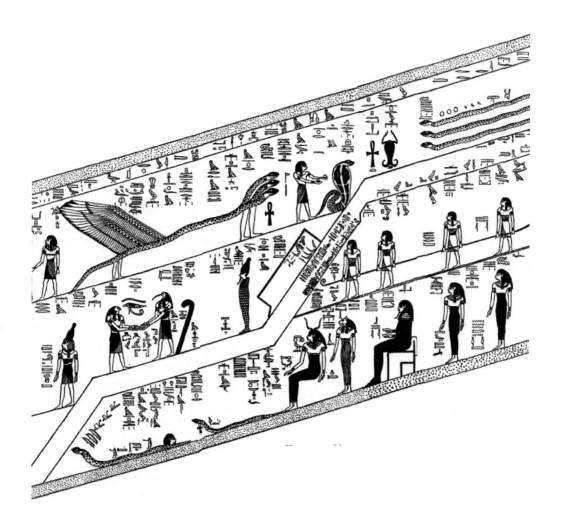

Mid to Lower Register
Path and Final Gate

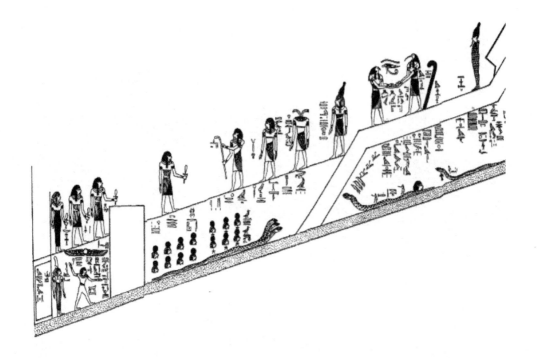

Wat s2tat a2qt n(ty) Jnpw h2r.s r jmn h2at Wsjr.
Wat s2tat n r Jmh2t; Nwt H4awt.
Mds n Nh2h2.

Lunar Sequence

(right to left)

Alterer

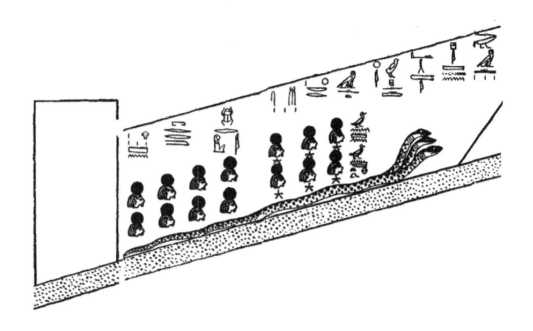

Mnmnw. Ss2mw p(w){y} s2ta n Jmh2t.[18] Jw psd jm.s ra2 nb r msjt H3prj prr m h2rw Mnmnw, h2rj.h3r H3prj.

---

18   Note the ambiguity of *ss2mw n*, which could be read both as "who leads to" and "image of." .

Kepri and Maat

H3prj h2tp.f m smh3.f n nt2r sab-s2wt jmy h2rt pt. Maa2t.

Ra's Procession, Part One: Lower and Middle Registers

Text for Middle Register Left of Gate and Bottom Register

Wnn.sn m sh3r pn, m ss2m.sn n d2(w)t.sn jmnw(t) n H2r h2r wat tn d2srt nt jmnt s2taw. Wnn.sn jmyw-r wat dsrt nt a2q jmnt nt dwat. Ntsn saa(w) Jnpw m ss2mw.f n st2a, a2pj.n.f h2r.sn m ta dsr.

119

Two Serpents Guarding the Path

H2knt. Wnn.s m sh3r pn m sawt nt wat tn. H2kn.s m h2rwy.s(y) n ss2mw a2a
   nt(y) jm.s.

Jmn. Wnn.f m sh3r pn, jmy-r n wat tn s2tawt nt Jmh2t. N s2m.n.f r st nb ra2 nb,
   anh3.f m h3rw nt2rw wat tn.

Five Deities

Wnn.sn m sh3r pn m maa n H2r (or śs2m jrjw.n wat).[19] *A2h2a2.sn m ta r wat tn s2tat nt Jmh2t, a2qt.sn, nt sp tpy m ta.*

T2st Wpt, H2ngt, Bn(t){ny}, S2at(y)t, Mt2nyt.

---

19 The glyph could be read either way. Both senses are applicable.

Snake Bier

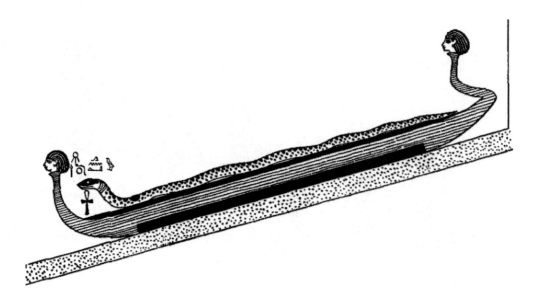

Jw Ra2 na2w[20] h2d2.

*Wnn.f m sh3r pn m wja.f saa(w) Jmh2t. A2h2a2.f r wat s2tat nt Jmh2t, a2nh3.f
m h3rw mdw tpw n wja.f*

---

20   I have retained the enigmatic spelling here because of the play on words. We could read this
     word as the adjective *na2a2*, "smooth;" the verb *na2j*, "to travel;" or the noun *na2w*, "snake."
     All three meanings are appropriate.

Friends of Horus

Ss2mw A2nh3, Jnj-H2rt, Wd2-Mdw, Nbt A2nh3.

Gods of the Wedjat Procession

H2tp, Wad2 H2r, H2ry D2bat.f, St2nj H2at.

Aw-A2, Skry, Wt2sw.

Mst Wsjr, Ma2nh3ty.

Ra's Procession, Part Two: Middle and Upper Registers

Path and Midway Gate

Wat st2at nt R-St2aw, sba nt2r; {n} s2m.n n.f sn, h3rw.f pw sd2m.sn.
Wat nt a2qt h4at nt Skr H2ry S2a2j.f: ss2m s2ta n maa, n ptr.
Mds maw[21] ta.

---

21   I have kept the enigmatic spelling for the sake of the pun: we can read this either as
maa2w, "which leads through," or as *maw*, "new."

Text over Sun's Barque

Sqdd nt2r pn a2a h2r sn m sh3r pn. Jn sd2t tpy-r n wja.f ss2m sw m nn n mt2nw s2taw jwty maa.f ss2m.sn. Dwj.f n.sn r haw.sn, h3rw.f pw sd2mw.sn.

Dragging the Boat

Dwn Maawt,[22] H2ry Wart, Jry Nfrt, S2tawy.

---

22 *Maa2t* here means "tow rope," but the ostrich feather determinative gives the an added sense.

Solar Barque and Crew

Dm Wat.

Wpj-Wawt, Sja, Nb(t) Wja, Jwf, H2r H2knw, Ka Maat, Nhs, Hw.

Four Deities

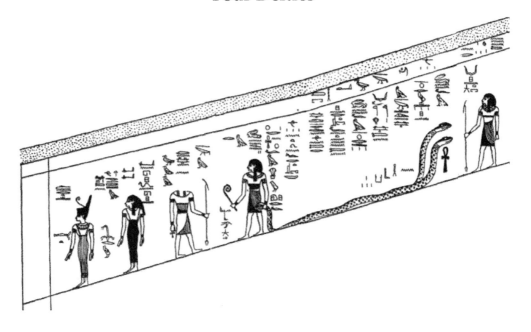

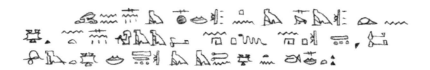

Wnn.sn m sh3r pn m ss2mw jrj(w).n wat (or H2r).[23] *Ntsn saa Nhp*[24] *nhp ta, dd
  wat r s2ta m mt2n dsrt{t}*

Mh2t, Rswt, H2knw Tp.

*Wpj Dwat wnn.f m sh3r pn m ss2m jrj(w).n H2r (or wat), wpj.f nt2rwy h2r
  mt2n.*

---

23 Both readings possible.

24   The reading of *Nhp* as the name of the serpent boat is suggested by the snake
    determinative: Hornung points out that *Nhp* is the name of a snake-headed bier in
    the Book of Gates.

Neheb-Kaw Group

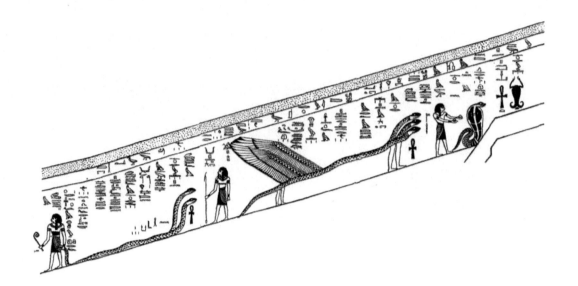

Sereqet

Srqt anh3t: wnn.s m sh3r pn, a2h2a2.s (r) R-St2aw, tp(yt) n(t) wat tn.

Thoth

Wpj(w) nt2rwy: wnn.f m sh3r pn, m ss2m n H2r d2s.f, wpj.f ss2m wat dsrt.

Winged Neheb-Kaw

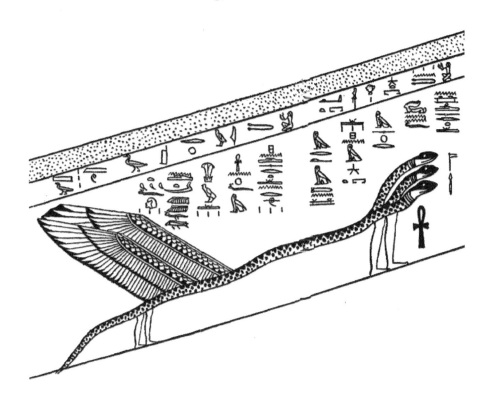

Nt2r a2a a2nh3 wnn.f m sh3r pn m dwat, jmy-r mt2n pn dsr n R-St2aw.
Anh3.f m t2aw n dmaty.fy, h4awt.f tpw.

Seth

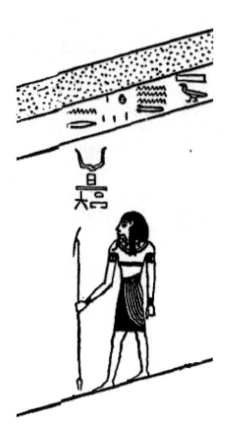

Neheb-Kaw

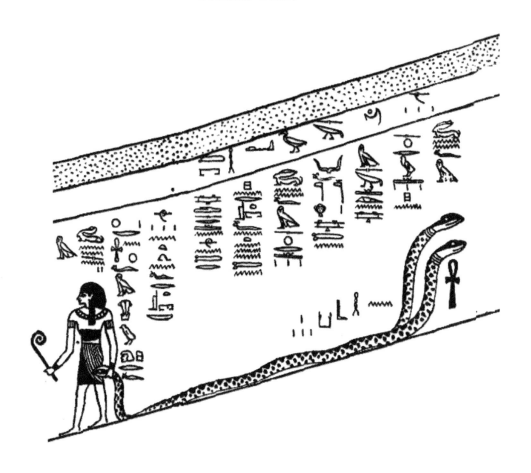

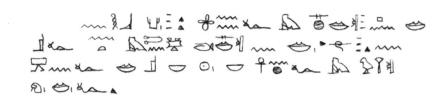

Nh2b Kaw wnn.f m sh3r pn r st.f nt mt2n dsr n R-St2aw. N s2m.n.f r st nb ra2 nb anh3.f m wd2 tp-r.f.

Neheb-Kaw in Human Form

A2ba Dwat

Entrance to the Hour

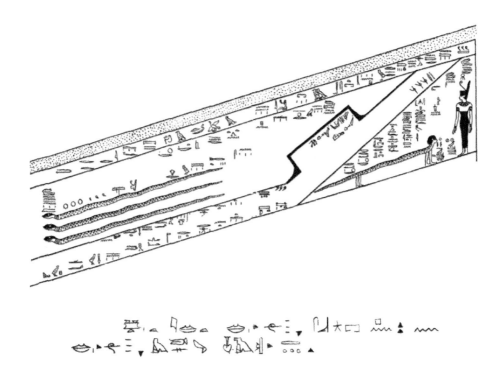

Wat jryt R-St2aw, sba pn; n R-St2aw, mds sma-ta.

Crowned Goddess and Guardian of the Way

Wnn.s r wbn.

Tpy saw mt2n: wnn.f m jmy-r mt2n. N s2m.n.f r st nb ra2 nb.

Three Serpents

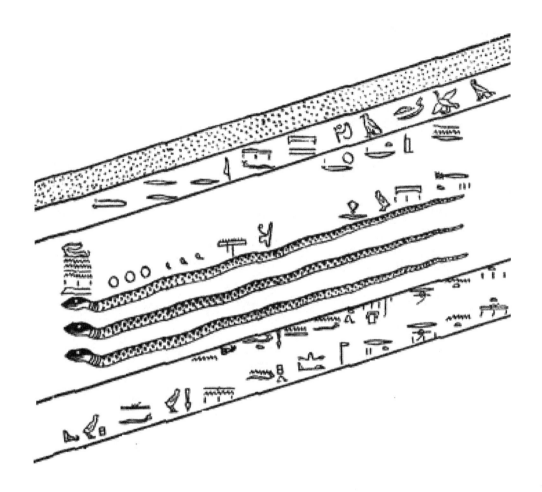

Jwfw Ra2 mnj h2ryw h2wt.sn: wn.sn m sh3r pn n s2m.sn r st nb ra2 nb.

Hour Five:

The Cave of Sokar

Poem

D2d-mdw jn nt2r pn a2a:[25]

Jmntt, dj a2.t2! Nfr mt2n wr, h4nw ta, wat jsw, h2tpw[26] nt2rw.j.
Srq.t2n, psd2t tw nt nt2rw h3prw m jwf.j,
tm-h3pr(w) n jrw.t2n, mn n h2nw.t2n.
Nd2.j (h2r.)t2n, nd2.t2n h2r.j. Nt2n wd2w n.j.
Dsr.{s}<t2>n h2r nd2-h2r.j m ta jmntt.

A2h2a2.n.t2n r mw.t2n, saj.n.t2n jdbw.t2n,
dj.t2n mh2t mh2yw jmyw Nnw, mnj.t2n sn n jdbw agbw.
Mw.t2n, n ws2r.sn. Qajt n(t) jdbw.t2n, n fak.sn.
Qa2h2 n.t2n rmn.t2n n d2aj-mw r a2pt(.f) h2r.t2n m h2tp.

---

25 In this hour there has been a particular effort to integrate the poem with the illustration. On tomb walls, the poem was divided into small sections and parcelled out among the parts of the image that illustrate them. I have here reassembled the complete poem.

26 The word *h2tpw* has its full range of meanings here.

Saw n.t2n hnw.t2n,
qajt n h3rw.t2n, maa2 n h2tywt.t2n,
jmn ss2mw pn²⁷ sa{a}w.t2n.
Wpj.n.t2n dmawt.t2n, jrj.n(.t2n) jrw.t2n
r a2pjt.j h2r.t2n m h2tp.²⁸

J d2sr, d2sr n.j rmn.k, wn n.j ph2r.k,
d2sr n.k rmn.k, wn ph4r.k, h2rwy.ky m ta!
N stj.k wj, n ss2r.k r ntyw m h3t.j
r a2pt.j h2r.k m h2tp.

J smaw jryw nmt, a2h2a2yw h2r qnjt mwtw:
h3pr n mdw.t2n, ss2p n h2kaw.t2n,
spd n baw.t2n, was2 n sh3mw.t2n!
Nd2(.t2n) h3ftyw, sh2tm.t2n mwtyw,
s2a2d.t2n s2wt, h2tmyw, njkyw — mwtw(.t2n) nb(w){.t2n}.

---

27 The text has *pn ss2mw*, which I reverse with Hornung.

28 We should recognize (as the illustrator has) the allusion to Isis and Nephthys, and scrupulously maintain the text as written. *Lectio difficilior praeferenda.*

Ntt2n nd2-h2r Wsjr, sd2mw "mdw-h2r" Wnn-Nfr.
Spd n sfw.t2n, qnt n nmwt.t2n,
t2s n sws2wt.t2n, a2wy.t2n h2r ss2mw jmyw.t2n r a2pjt.j h2r.t2n m h2tp.

D2d-mdw jn nt2rw dwatyw n nt2r pn a2a:

M h2tp sp sn, nb a2nh3! M h2tp, h2tp Jmntt!
M h2tp, wn ta! M h2tp, wba ta!
M h2tp, jmy pt! M h2tp, h2tp nnt!
M h2tp, maa2-h3rw! Nb psd2t, m h2tp!

Wn n.k ta rmn, maa2 n.k Nfrt wawt.s. H3rw.k, Ra2, n Wsjr, d2wj.k, Ra2, n ta Skr, a2nh3 Skr h2ry s2a2j.f.

Mj n H3prj, Ra2! Ra2, mj n H3prj!
Nfrt, jnj n.tn nfrt sa2rt n H3prj!
Dj.f a2 n Ra2, maa2.f wawt s2tawt n Ra2-H2r-Ah3ty,
Pt m h2tp sp sn, Ra n jmntt nfrt.

(D2d-mdw) jn nt2r pn a2a {h2r tp qrrt tn}[29]

Sja.kwy ss2mw.k pn, Skr, jmn, s2ta.
D2wj n.k, (n) ah3.k: mdw.j n.k, h2knw.k jm.sn.[30]
Ast n ss2mw.k, nt2r a2a, n h4at.k. Swt saa(t).f.[31]

---

29 Evidently an addition to better integrate the lines with the image.

30 Lit. "My words are to you, your praises are (contained) in them (in my words)."

31 This last phrase I take as a participial statement beginning with the archaic independent pronoun. The *f* refers back to *ss2mw*.

D2d-mdw jn {nn n}[32] nt2rwt n nt2r pn a2a:

Jj Ra2 m h2tp n Dwat, maa2 wat Ra2
m wja.f jmy-ta, m d2t.f. h2tm.tw h3ftyw.f n.{k}(f) jm.
Jmntt, Ra2, h2tp.k jm.s, (j)a2r.k n pt m ba a2a h2r tp sh3mw ah3t. St2aw.k, h3pr
st2aw.k, maa2-h3rw.k, dr h3ftyw.k!

D2d-mdw jn nt2r pn a2a:

S2sp n.t2n mdw.t2n, (t)wa n.t2n (h2r) d2a2mw.t2n, rhn n.t2n (h2r) amsw.t2n,
a2h2a2.t2n n[33] baw.t2n, h2ms.t2n n h2tp.t2n.
Ntsn jryw awt t, nbw h3rwt m jmntt.
Ast, dj.s n.t2n jmntt—h2tp.s h2r.t2n.
A2h2a2.n jryw.tn, mwtw.t2n, r a2pt.j h2r.t2n m h2tp.

---

32 *n* meaning "because of."

33 *n* meaning "because of."

Wat s2tat nt Jmh2t,[34] *st2a nt2r pn h2r.s: wnn.s h4r(t) bwt Nhs, rwty jmntt.*

Wat s2tat nt ta Skr a2t.n Ast h2r.s r wnn m-h3t sn.s:
wnn.s mh2t m ns sd2ty, tpt-r Ast, n a2pj.n nt2rw, ah3w, mwtw h2r.s.

Wat s2tat nt ta Skr jmntyw, sta2w nt2r pn, jwtt apj{p} nt2rw ah3w mwtw h2r.s:
wnn.s mh2t m ns sd2ty, tpt-r n(t) wam{m}t.[35]

---

34   *Jmh2t*, originally a name for the Nile's imagined underground source, became a euphemism for the graveyard, which one might English as "spring of renewal."In this hour the normal spelling (maimed in Hour Four) is restored, and so I now give the word a more positive rendering.

35   *Wamt*, "she who roasts," is Isis in serpent form: so suggests the parallel line beginning *wnn.s* immediately above, and the standard use of a rearing cobra as a goddess determinative.

H2d2 n nwt jryt nt2r pn m jrty tp nt2r a2a—
h2ay rdwy(.fy) m qab nt2r a2a saw.f ss2mw.f![36]

Jw sd2m.tw h3rw h3t m nwt tn m-h3t a2pp nt2r pn a2a h2r.s{n},
my h3rw hmhmt nt h2rt m ns2njt.s.

---

36   Literally: "A brightness (comes) to the underworld of this god (Sokar) from the eyes
     in the head of a great god (Ra-Horus); a shining of legs (emerging) from the belly of
     the great god (Time-Serpent, Kepri) who kept his (Osiris') form."

Introduction

St2aw nt2r pn a2a h2r wawt maa2wt nt Dwat m h2ry "Qrrt S2tat nt Skr h2ry
    S2a2j.f:"
n ma(w), n ptr(w) ss2mw pn s2ta n ta h4ry h2a2w nt2r pn.
Jw jmyw nt2r pn, sd2m.sn h3rw Ra2 d2wj.f r haw nt2r pn.

Rn n sba nt njwt tn "A2h2a2 Nt2rw," rn n qrrt nt2r pn "Jmntt,"
rn n wnwt tn nt grh2 ss2mt nt2r pn a2a "Ss2mt h2ryt-jb Wja.s."

Wawt s2tawt nt jmntt, sbaw n a2qt jmnt, bw dsr n ta Skr: jwf d2t m h3prw
    tpy(w):
rh3 baw jmyw dwat, jrywt.sn n jmyt wnwt m rnw.sn s2taw! N{t} rh3(w), n
    ma(w), n ptr(w) ss2mw pn n H2r d2s.f!

Jw jrj.tw nn my ss2mw pn nty m ss2 m jmntt nt Dwat h2r rsyt a2t jmnt.
Jw rh3 st m h2tp, ba.f h2tp.f m h2tp Skr. N dn.n h3mywt h4at.f. Jw ph4rt ntsn
    tp-ta.

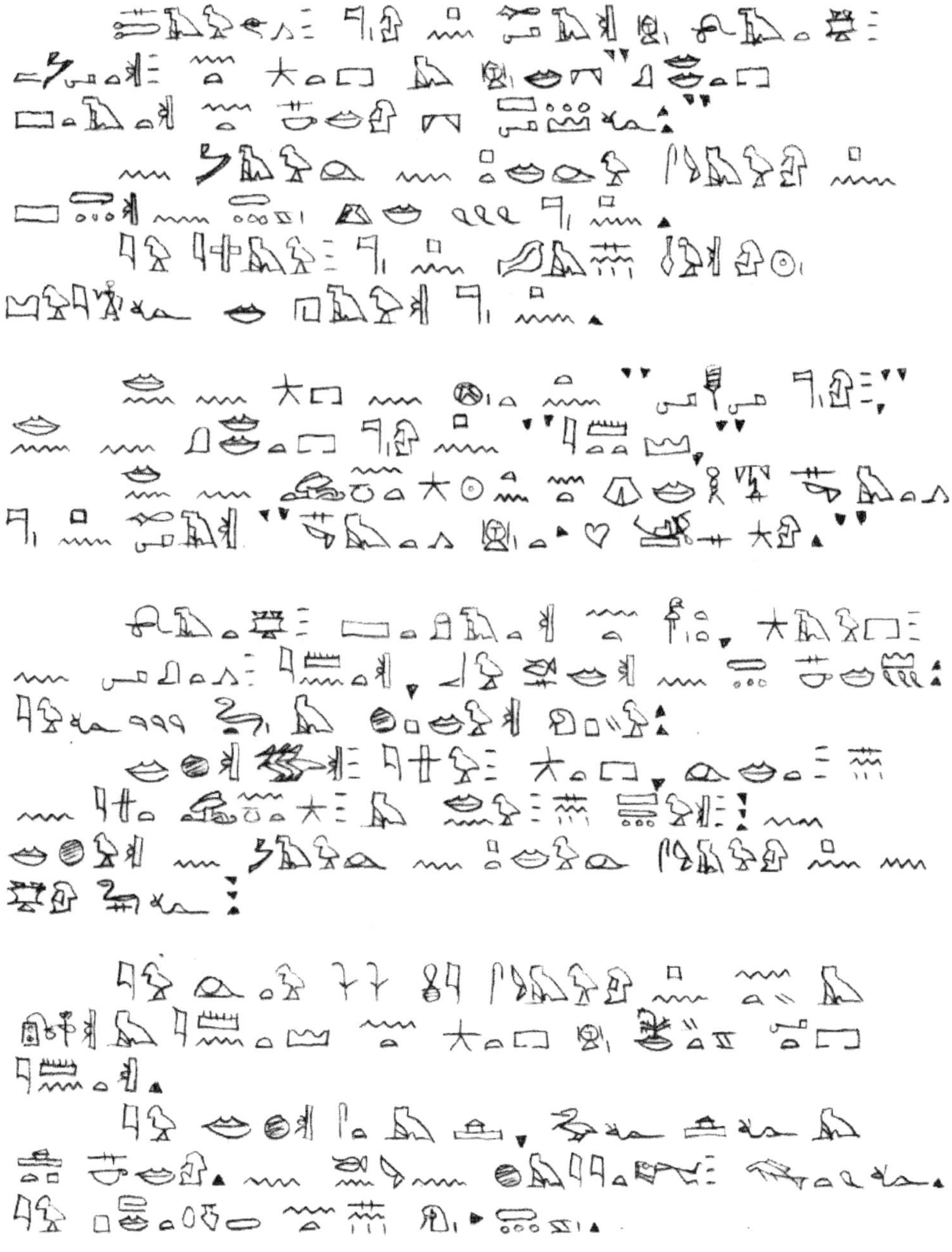

Complete Image of the Hour

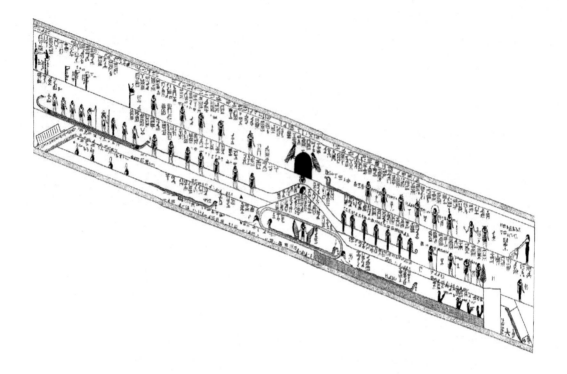

159

Complete Image: second from left

Complete Image: third from left

Complete Image: center left

Complete Image: second from right

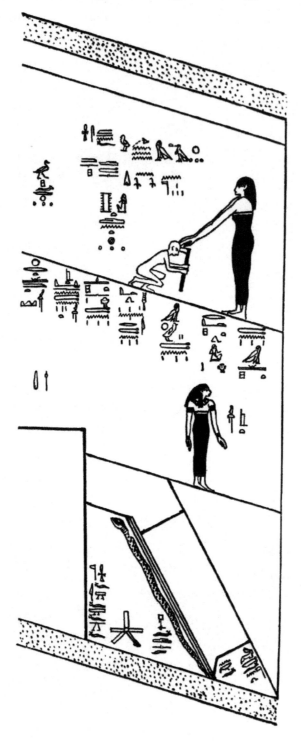

Detail from Center

The Ennead

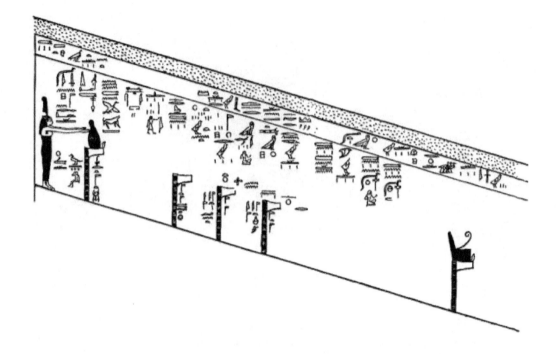

H2n{w}{p}n nn n ntt2rw m dwat: wnn.sn, m sh3r pn.

H2wt-H2r Jwrt[37] (m) H4rd,
Nt2ryt rsyt H3prj,
Nt2ryt S2w, Nt2ryt Tfnt,
Nt2ryt Gb, Nt2ryt Nwt,
Nt2ryt Wsjr, Nt2ryt Ast, Nt2ryt Nbt-H2wt, Nt2ryt Mh2yt H2r-Dwaty.

---

37 The enigmatic writing of this name is particularly delphic: *Ra2* (=*H2r*) + *h2a2w* ("body") + *t2* (= *t*) + *wr* +*ta* gives us *H2r-h2a2w-t2* (honorific transposition) *wr-ta,* and so the name as I have transliterated it.

Waters of Rebirth

Wnn.sn m jryw nt mhyw m dwt. Jrjt.sn: a2pjt wja.

Pawty Nwt, A2nh3 Jb, Saw Jdbw, Jry Mw Mh2w.

Isis and Nephthys on the Tomb

Jnpw hnw, grh2, Ast, Nbt-H2wt.

Two Headed Serpent

A2nh3.f m h3rw Ra2 ra2 nb, jwty jw.n.f r st nbt nt Dwat. Wnn.f r hn H3prj.

Punishers

Punishers Text

Ntsn a2h2a2(w) h2r qnjt mwtw m Dwat. Jrjt sn pw, samt h4awt mwtw m hhw n r.sn m h4rt-hrw.

Ba Pf Jry Mwtw, A2nn h2r Sph2{t}, Jnj Maa2t, A2by, A2m, Mst, Snd2 n.f Jmntyw, (Rdj) H2tp Nt2rw.

Jw rh3.s m swa h2r.s m h2tp. A2nh3.s m snfw mwtw, m spdd(w).n n.s nn n nt2rw.

H2mjt, dnt Mwtw.

Middle Register

Sun Boat and Those Who Tow It.

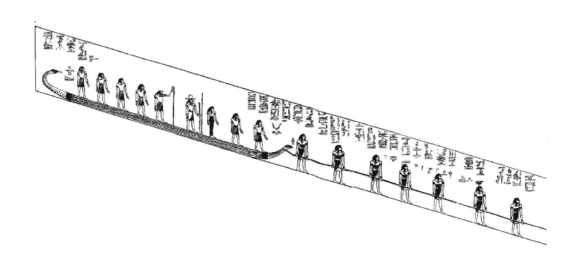

Sqdd nt2r pn a2a m st2aw h2r qrrt tn m wja.f jmy-ta "A2nh3 Baw."

Nt2rw Dwatyw. Jrjt.sn pw st2a nt2r pn h2r qrrt Skr.

Kepri

A2h2a2 nt2r pn h2r tp nt2rt tn,
wd2-mdw.f m ta Skr ra2 nb.
Jn H3prj jmy pr.f maa2 nfrt n st2aw h2r tp qrrt tn r h2tp.f, (H2r, h2r) wat nt
    Dwat.[38]

Jwf Ast h2ryt s2a2j Skr.

---

38   Triple pun: the text has only the word *wat*, which does not yeild an intelligible
    phrase. However *wat*, the "road" ideogram, is also used for the name Horus (*H2r*),
    and this is identical in sound with the word for "upon" (*h2r*).

Towing Goddesses

Sqdwt m st2ta jn h2m n nt2r pn a2a, ss2p jn nn n nt2rwt.

Nt2rwt st2awt Ra2 m Dwat h2r qrrt tn: jrjt.sn pw, st2aw nt2r pn a2a r h2tp.f, wja.f, jmy Nwn m Dwat.

Providers of Food

Wnn.sn m sh3r pn: d2ad2at pw snmt awt m qrrt tn.

Ast Jmntt, Wd2-Mdw, H2r Hqaty, Jnj H2tp(w), H2ry Jrw.

Lower Register

Gate

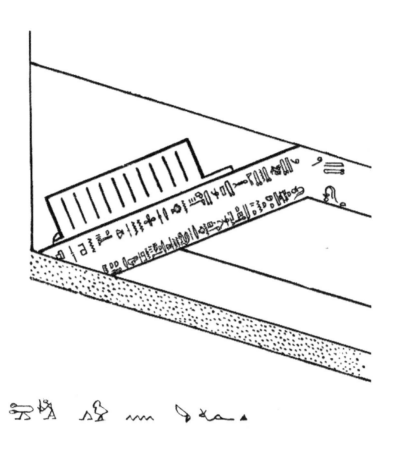

Jt2j.f jw n mds.f.

179

Fire Spirits

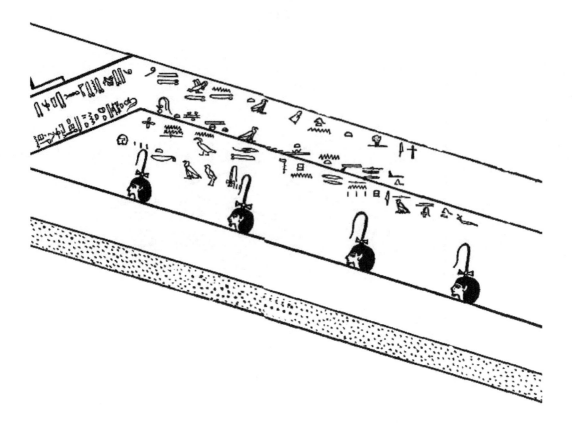

Tpw tkaw.

Wnn.sn m-ḥ3t nt2r pn: jrjt.sn pw, samt nmtwt h3ftyw.f

Carrier of Prayers

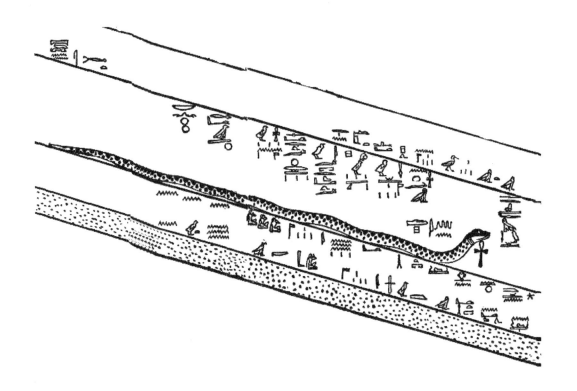

D2sr Tp.

A2nh3.f m h3rw nt2rw tpyw ta. Jw.f a2q.f prj.f sa2r.f h3rwt a2nh3w n nt2r pn a2a ra2 nb, n(n) maa.

The Womb of the Earth

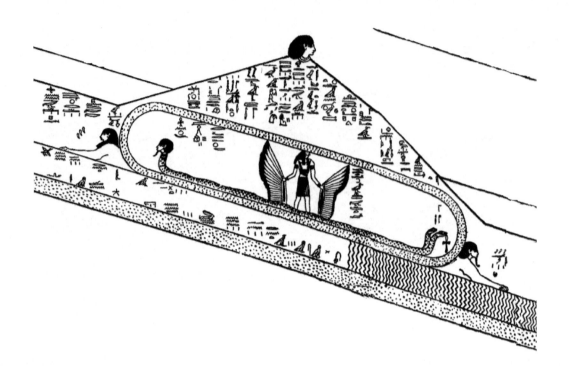

Jwf.

Aker

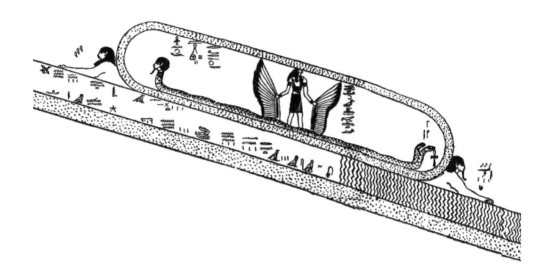

Srq.f m h3rw ntr a2a. Jrjt.f pw: sawt ss2m(w).f.[39]

Akr saa jwf s2ta ta skry.

Wnn ss2m pn m sh3r pn m kkw smaw.

---

39 The *(w)* here is added because we could read the word as either *ss2m* ("process") or
ss2mw ("form").

Sokar

Jwf, Skr h2r s2a2j.f

Hour Five: Center

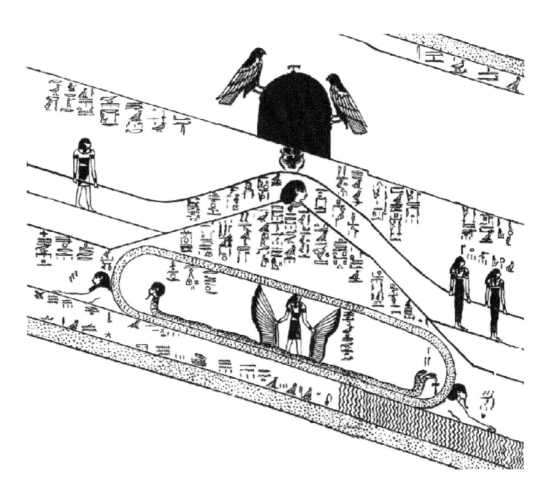

A2nh3.f m t2aw tpy-r.f ra2 nb. Jrjt.f pw, sat ss2m(w).f[40]
— nt2r a2a wpj d2nh2wy, sab s2w.

---

40   Literally: "He (the snake) lives by the breath from his (Ra's) mouth every day. His task is to watch over his (Ra's) process (or form)."

Scorcher

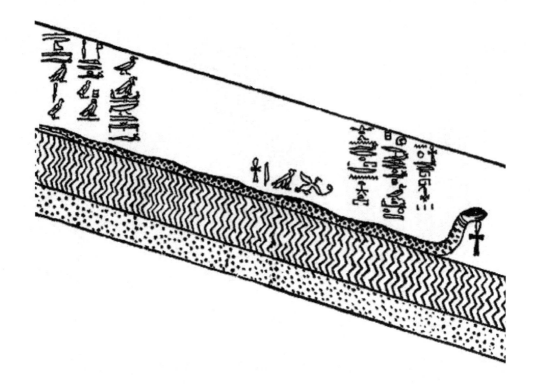

Wam: a2nh3.f m hh tp-r.f. Jrjt.f pw, sat nwt, jwty jw.n.f r st nb n Dwat.

Amun

Nt2rw h4ryw{t} ss2mw s2ta n Skr h2ry s2a2j.f.

Ss2m(w).sn m prjt jm.sn, m d2t.sn d2s.sn:
wnn.sn m-h3t nt2r pn a2a n ma(w).n jrt.

Lake of Fire

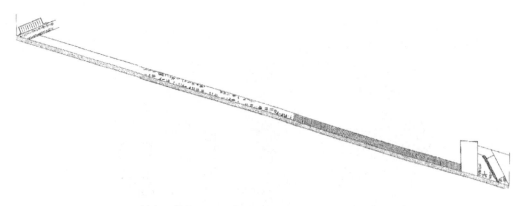

Nwt jakbyw, nt2rw jmyw Jmh2t:

n a2pj.n wja h2r.sn,
n sh3m dwatyw m mw.sn wnn m h4rt-nt2r pn.
Wnn mw.sn r ntyw jm.s m sd2t.

Serpent at Hellgate

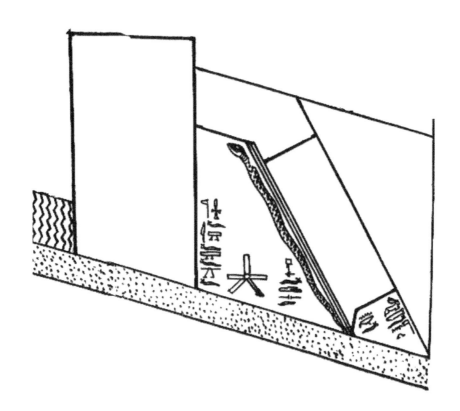

Nt2r a3nh3: jw.f s2m.f jj.f sbj.f wba.f ds.

Printed in Great Britain
by Amazon